OFF COLOUR

JACKIE KAY

Off Colour

BLOODAXE BOOKS

Copyright © Jackie Kay 1998

ISBN: 1 85224 420 8

First published 1998 by
Bloodaxe Books Ltd,
Highgreen,
Tarset,
Northumberland NE48 1RP.

Second impression 2002

www.bloodaxebooks.com
For further information about Bloodaxe titles
please visit our website or write to
the above address for a catalogue.

Bloodaxe Books Ltd acknowledges
the financial assistance of Northern Arts.

northern
arts

Cover printing by J. Thomson Colour Printers Ltd, Glasgow.

Printed in Great Britain by
Cromwell Press Ltd, Trowbridge, Wiltshire.

for my parents

Acknowledgements

Acknowledgements are due to the editors of the following publications where some of these poems first appeared: *The Fire People* (Payback Press, 1998), *Independent on Sunday*, *Making for Planet Alice* (Bloodaxe Books, 1997), *New Statesman*, *The Observer*, *Penguin Modern Poets 8* (1996) and *Poetry Review*. 'Christian Sanderson' was published as a Prospero Poets pamphlet in 1996, and 'Sabbath' was made into a television feature film with Bill Paterson by BBC Wales and shown by BBC 2. Some poems were also broadcast on *The Afternoon Shift* on BBC Radio 4.

Contents

Where It Hurts

Let me tell you what like it is.
It's a great muckle hand inside my guts, clawing.
Or a camshachle crow; beak at my kidneys.
See the way yon thing over there is moving?
Well, it moves like that. Like a verb.
There's the thump, the weight falling – *here*.
Give me your hand; that's it,
across my chest. Heavy, like the battle o' Culloden.
Oh Christ yes. Don't kid yourself; I'm not kidding.
The body is a bloody battlefield.

These knees of mine are full of fluid.
See, feel. Don't be gentle. *Push*, prod.
God, you can almost hear the sea in my knees;
there's so much water, slapping, slopping,
slobbering at the shore. I'm away the trip.
You could cross the water; you could speed bonny boat
and still not reach me – bird on a wing.
My illnesses just keep coming; going out-in, in-out.
I've been sick since time immemorial.
Since the days of the plague, the black death;

since the rain of the frogs, cats and dogs.
I could throw myself up and never come back.
Chuck myself into the sea, the North Sea.
The black water would gulp me down, whole.
I don't think I'd so much as wave,
I'm that sickened with myself. Sick.
Sick. Sick. Sick to death of being sick.
Always spoiling everybody's fun.
Lying down when people are up and about.
In a dark room, when people are laughing in light.

I go to the Doctor but what does the Doctor say?
He looks at me as if I were a germ, a sudden outbreak.
When did you start feeling this way? he mumbles,
already scribbling my sentence, my fate.
What's the disease inheritance? What's in the family?
What odd traits have been passed down? Background?
Christ! I come from a long line of sufferers.
We lived with live-in disease-ridden beasts.
We caught rabies, had babies, passed madness down.
We clenched our crossed teeth.

Sick to the back Scotch teeth.
I could spit my teeth out on stone floor –
too many scones, treacle scones, fruit scones,
currant loaf, malt loaf. Crumble. Too much sponge,
light sponge, heavy sponge. Dumpling. Shortbread –
too many rhubarb tarts, custard creams, eclairs.
My blood sugar is soaring. My tongue is so sugary
I flatter my enemies. My healthy, blooming enemies.
I say sweet things when I want to weep and spit.
They tell me I'm looking well; lies – I'm peelie-wally!

Today people tell the sick they look well.
A leper never had to suffer compliments.
If I could say I had consumption, spotted fever,
cholera, smallpox, tuberculosis, apoplexy, let's say,
any classic would do: hookworm, bookworm, bubonic plague.
If my house had to be fumigated, smoked with sulphur;
if I could suffer a rosie on my face, eggs in my groin;
somebody might take me seriously, might listen.
If I could have a day, an ordinary day,
away from the worry – the body – I would be happy.

How can I be happy when loss is greeting round the corner?
Let my body fill with poison, bacteria, culture
while the workers go to the pictures or opera;
culture with a choc ice, tub of vanilla.
Let my body swirl with my hosts,
let the wee life-forms dance and flounce,
shaking their big bellies; sobbing, multiplying.
Madame Butterfly, Tosca, Treponema.
You clever bastard, bacteria, always a new story.
Oh bacteria, bacteria; *wild*, the sea moans.

Up to here. I've had it. *Here.* C'Mere.
I'm a guillotine at my own neck. Chop.
My neck is as stiff as a donkey's cock.
I can only turn round this far – look.
It's got that bad I've started to swear.
I've begun to think in obscenities, I can't stop – cunt.
How did I get like this? So far away from myself.
I used to love ballads, folksongs.
I will go I will go when the fighting is over.
But the fighting of the body is never over.

The stars are white cells. There is no beauty.
When you are sick like me,
day in day out, sunrise, sundown, it spreads.
Like the illness spreads. Across fields, memories.
My eyes see right through the body to the bad bits.
The scary bits cowering inside the flesh.
Growths that people don't yet know about.
I can see it coming. It's not just me.
The tinge of green, the yellow eyes, the shaky
hands, the puffy face, the tell-tale signs.

True, true. Some are braver than me: I'm not
brave. I've gone from one time to another
puking, spewing; bloated, swollen.
Sick as a parrot, a gambler, a joke, a dog, a mind.
Sick as a simile, sick (sic), a poet, a plant.
Drooping, limp, languid, flaccid, fatigued.
Bored to death, belching, burping, breaking wind.
Oh the terrible ennui, the listlessness of illness.
Oh the repetitive answers: 'How are you?' 'Not so good.
Could be better. Seen better days, Don't ask.'

You can't say I haven't tried everything.
Hypnotherapy, acupuncture, homeopathy, reflexology.
My tarots read. My chart done. See that astrology!
Psycho analytical psycho therapy. Alexander's Technique.
Moved my three-piece suite. Rubbed seaweed on my feet.
Something meant to unblock my energy. Synergy?
Brown rice and bananas for breakfast, dinner, tea.
Nat Mur? Wasn't that my remedy? The sea in me.
My homeopathic personality: I hoard painful memories;
I nurse grievances; I don't forgive; I take offence easily.

11

Don't say I haven't tried to be well. I've tried.
I've smiled. But what's a smile but an attempt to hide tears.
Many's the time, I've gone out unwell, near collapsing.
A burning pain straight down the middle of the throat.
Dead centre. Like somebody's lit a line of gunpowder.
The sick headache tightening the screws. Zigzags.
My moods swing. My sinuses scream. I look like a hag.
There's not a pain I haven't had.
I could paint the pains on a big white sheet.
The weary wabbit world of the worried unwell.

It's not just me is it? I'm not the only one.
Were we always this ill? Was I?
When we die is the sensation heavy, light?
I'll die a weighty, hefty, heaving death.
Other light people around me might take flight
like graceful swallows. But I'll be a huge pig
squealing. A fucking great buffalo roaring.
What a big bitter pill to swallow
– will it be red, will it be yellow?
After all I've been through. A great thumping death.

A fucking great fucking big death.

The Shoes of Dead Comrades

On my father's feet are the shoes of dead comrades.
Gifts from the comrades' sad red widows.
My father would never see good shoes go to waste.
Good brown leather, black leather, leather soles.
Doesn't matter if they are a size too big, small.

On my father's feet are the shoes of dead comrades.
The marches they marched against Polaris. UCS.
Everything they ever believed tied up with laces.
A cobbler has replaced the sole, the heel.
Brand new, my father says, look, feel.

On my father's feet are the shoes of dead comrades.
These are in good nick. These were pricey.
Italian leather. See that. Lovely.
He always was a classy dresser was Arthur.
Ever see Wullie dance? Wullie was a wonderful waltzer.

On my father's feet are the shoes of dead comrades.
It scares me half to death to consider
that one day it won't be Wullie or Jimmy or Arthur,
that one day someone will wear the shoes of my father,
the brown and black leather of all the dead comrades.

Crown and Country

When you come to our country
you will realise we are big on dentistry:
at the border your mouth will be opened, flossed
and an elegant silver filling stamped into D10.
Then you will catch the hygienic autobus, *Tooth*
Fairy Express smiling the improved smile of our people

who all know dentures are more crucial
than culture. We do not talk much, we say
cheese; pints of creamy gleaming teeth,
pouring out our white grins, our gold caps; smirks.
Just across the border, people have hellish holes,
gaping gaps, rotten roots, abscesses.

We identify people by their bite.
The lower class have most unusual bites.
They are sick to the back teeth.
At 2 a.m. on a hot dusty night in out town
you will hear the fraught percussion
of the entire population grinding its teeth.

Our dentists are the richest in the world,
mining our gobs of gold. They love the old;
the ones who finally succumb to receding gums,
to teeth falling haplessly out like hailstones.
Be careful of the wind; it can make your mouth fly wide.
All along this natural canal, you will note,
our wild poppies pout; lush red lips.

Teeth

(i.m. Joy Gardner)

This is X who has all her own teeth.
Her mother is horrified by this.

Look into her mouth. She still has them.
Perfect pearls. Milk stones. Pure ivory.

Not a filling, no receding gums.
X was a woman with a lively

smile. Since she was a girl. No dark holes.
Her mother wore, still does, false teeth. Tusks,

badly fitted, left something unsaid –
a tiny gap between tooth and gum.

Her mum's teeth, in a glass tumbler, swam
at night: a shark's grin; a wolf's slow smirk.

What upsets her mother now, oddly,
is this: X had such beautiful lips.

This morning the men broke in – 8 a.m.
X was wearing her dressing gown, white

towelling. They came wearing her number
on their arms. *Did you know*, her mother says,

they taped my daughter's mouth to choke her
screams. They covered her mouth in white tape.

The small boy pulled at the sharp trousers.
He was soundless. The big men flung him

into that grey corner. His voice burst.
He will stand there, that height, forever, see

those minutes grab and snatch and repeat
themselves. The men in plain-clothes have claws;

they attack his mother like dogs, gagging her,
binding her, changing her into someone

else. He will watch her hands smash and thrash.
His hands making a church, then a tall

steeple. He crosses his fingers. Squeezes them.
His hands wet themselves. He is five years old.

He knows his address. He knows his name.
He has ten fingers. He count them again.

This is X who has all her own teeth.
Came to this country with her own teeth.

Soundbites will follow. Lies will roll
tomorrow. The man with the abscess

will say she had a weak heart. High blood.
Illegal. Only doing his job.

Fill it in. Write it down. Bridge the gap.
Give him a stamp of approval: silver

or gold or NHS, she resisted arrest;
there's your cause of death. On a plate.

She was wrong. Give her a number. Think
of a number. Take away the son.

The Black Chair

Now I am inside the room
after all the dreaded waiting;
a woman is kinder, more gentle.

So you have me open my mouth;
I open it gladly for you.
Tiny mirrors, softly you tell

your assistant the language of ivory:
my vowels, my consonants, my country.
It is all unfathomable to me

but it sounds beautiful, rhythmical.
I could be crumbling, spotted with decay;
maybe need a filling, a cap, root canal.

My abscess is a mystery, a swollen book.
You tuck me up and put me to sleep.
My soft swollen gums are stroked, all red,

my tiny dark holes prodded
by one of your strange foreign instruments.
They lie at my side now gleaming

sharp as a family,smiling in a silver album.
I am laid back on your director's chair –
the pink glass of champagne at my side.

Every so often I rise for a moment
like a woman rising from a dream of the dead
like a woman standing up on a horse

to drink and swirl and spit and watch
my own frothy blood spin and disappear.
You say good, good, you're doing fine,

again, again, till your voice is a love song
and every cavity an excuse for meeting;
floss is the long length of string

that keeps us parted. My mouth is parted.
You are in it with your white gloved hands
I have not eaten garlic for weeks.

But you don't need to pull any teeth
alas, no molars to come out in your hands
no long roots, no spongy bits of gum.

We won't go that far. No. It's surface stuff,
really. Not nearly as deep as you or I could go.
You'll polish them. You'll give the odd amalgam.

You'll x-ray. You'll show me the photo.
I'll look at my own teeth on the white screen
They tell me nothing about myself.

My teeth, speechless.
Rootless pearls, anonymous white things.
I need you to tell me about myself.

Will the gaps widen with the years?
Do you know the day my grandmother died was hot, baking?
Can you tell I like sex from the back row?

I'd like it now, on this black chair that you move
up or down, bringing me back to life
telling me in a cheerful voice, I'm done.

Plague

Our black door has a white X.
Next door but one has a white X.

59, 64, 65, 62, 68, and, fresh this morning,
58. The curly headed twins just turned four.

Our white X on our black door seems bigger
than 64. Two of us are blighted.

When I come home
the first thing I see is the white X.

I can't help myself.
Once I've looked,

I can't stop. Even inside with
all the terrible breathing

and the smell of the terrible breathing,
even inside, I still see X.

Last night, the shape of it falling asleep.
I don't sleep deep now. I sleep the sleep

of the dying's companion – fitful, fearful;
strange sudden still moments, long empty moments

and the loud breathless breathing.
I see X. It is the sign of the devil.

I pray for the breathing to stop.
I get up and watch my two shrunken sons;

outside the canny moon is hopeful.
Tonight, let them both go in one fell swoop.

And let me get that X off.
I've seen them come late with the black paint.

I want the X painted over *immediately.*
I want a plain black door

But 62 says, 'Once a marked
house, always a marked house.'

Even after it is painted over
you will still see it underneath,

62 says, smiling the strangest smile.
'It never goes you know, never.'

I looked and looked at 62
and all I could see was a black door.

62 whispered,'You can only see your own X then.'
She gripped my arm till it hurt.

I tell myself 62 has lost her mind.
Poor soul. But at night I hear the strange

sound of X crashing its awkward limbs
seeking the foreheads of my two dying sons.

X has a life of its own, I'm certain.
I hear the reckless, racy breathing.

I'm sweating now myself.
I'm losing weight. I can see our bones.

Our bones lying in the grave,silently arranged.
Our bones – one big white X lying on the black earth.

Race, Racist, Racism

1

Say the words came first.
Then the look followed.
Then it was the smell.
The fear of touch.

Say the field came first.
The rope came later.
Say there was a chair.
Say you didn't stand a chance.

2

When it happens it is down to me.
Entirely.
When it happens it is in my head.

I can say the names as well as you.
Lick the whip round my thick lips.
I can say the names as well as you.

It is all my fault for reading
something into nothing.
I know it is driving me insane.

I know this. I know dogs are men.
What are you saying?
You're saying nothing.

3

The country gave it to the people
as if it was a gift, wrapped in a coat.
It came off a boat. It was tall, fast.
When it first spoke, none of the people
knew what it was saying.

But when they caught on
out of their mouths came the gift's curse,
the slow slurred abuse, eyes staring,
till not a tongue in the country was clean,
till every mind was stained with its stain.

Who could help then?
What doctors could come to scrub a tongue
to disinfect a mind, to stop a plague.
Nobody knew how to cure it.

And it is true: many people died.

4

I am not black, said he.
I am not black, said he.
If you are not black, said I,
then what colour is the sky?

The sky is blue, said he.
The sky is blue, said he.
It does not matter one iota
that the sky is blue, said he.

There is no such thing as black, said he.
A pot is black, the earth, a shoe.
But not I, said he, not I.
I am not black, said he.

What colour will you be, said I?
What colour will you be?
I will be grey or brown or red.
I will be yellow or tan or beige.

I will be oak or hazelnut or coffee.
I will be toffee. I will be donkey.
But I will not be black, said he.
So you will be donkey, said I.

5

Here's the church and here's the steeple.
Open the door. They've burnt the people.

6

When the day breaks I will be there to break it.
When the new moon rises, I'll rise with it.
When the west wind blows, I'll puff and huff.
When the time comes, I'll say 'enough'.

I'll write 'The End' when it's the end of the story.

Say the words came first.

Virus *

Say the words
come first,   long
before the death,
before   the corpse;

say everybody knew
what would get them

                                              long
before they were born;

say it was like learning
              the alphabet: Anorexia,
Bulimia, CJD, diarrhoea, Ebola fever,
Forked tailed blood fluke, gonorrhoea,
say it was   it was written
                              **** in the stars ****
hookworm, influenza, jaundice, kidney stones,
leukaemia, malaria, neurosis, osteosclerosis,
plague, quarantine, rhinoviruses, sickle cell anaemia,
say it was all decided   long before
you   were   born,
tuberculosis, before u
knew you was spelt like that,
say you were targeted by a particular
virus, whooping cough X Y Z, corpse;
Yersina pestis, zoonoses, off by heart,
off by heart, x y z: corpse.

Hottentot Venus

They made a plaster cast of my corpse
took wax moulds of my genitals and anus,
my famous anomalous buttocks
till the last sigh in me left my body.

I made a noise I never heard before
when the man with the glinting knife
whispered 'posterity' and dissected my brain.
Not so long ago people paid handsomely

to see my rump, my apron, my non-European genitals.
Two shillings. I paced my cage, backwards,
an orang outang, forwards, a beast on a chain.
Men said the size of my lips were unnatural.

You can see the moulds of my genitals
at the Musée de l'Homme – Paris;
the rest of me is here now, Natural History Museum,
my brains, my woolly hair, my skeleton.

Some things I will never forget
no matter how I am divided up:
the look on a white lady's face
when she poked her parasol into my privates.

Her gloved hands. Her small stone eyes.
Her English squeal of surprise at my size.
My sigh is black. My heart is black.
My walk is black. My hide, my flanks. My secret.

My brain is the size of a black woman's brain.
When the gentleman prodded me with his cane,
he wanted to discover black tears falling
from my dark eyes. I tell no lies.

Then he called my tears crocodile tears.
What did he call my lips? Rubber? Blubber?
My country is a dream now. Or maybe it did not exist.
When they called me in, three men in suits,

They asked me in my own bush tongue
if I wanted to be exhibited in this fashion.
I said the English words I'd heard them say often.
Money. Freedom. My Boer keeper smiled.

He could still walk me, dance me
hold his stick to me. He promised me riches.
Bring in the literati, the artists, the famous.
Let them view the buttocks of the Hottentot Venus.

My heart inside my cage pounded like a single drum.
For eleven hours a day people came to see Saartjie Baartman.
I heard their laughter like money shaking in a tin.
On the wall I was framed: ugly, deformed, a cartoon.

I was wearing a thin skin coloured dress.
Hottentot Venus. Don't miss the Hottentot.
Now, what name have I got?
Sarah Bateman. Like an English woman. A great actress.

Somebody Else

If I was not myself, I would be somebody else.
But actually I am somebody else.
I have been somebody else all my life.

It's no laughing matter going about the place
all the time being somebody else:
people mistake you; you mistake yourself.

Christian Sanderson

Oor plan wis tae mak the clockmaker fu, fu
so's he wouldnie recognise me,
Bell or young Grace Thomson.
I sends oot fir mair malt whisky
bought wey the master clockmaker's shilling.
I'm shoor he wis expecting favours:
Grace wis the bait I used to lure him
doon the wynd they cry Hattie's close,
into the tenement. She's blonde and skinny
wey even, guid sized breasts.
I'm tae auld for a' that muck
an Bell wid rather pick a pocket or twa

fir a fine silk handkerchief
a guid gold watch or half a crown
than let a man like the clockmaker tak her.
And wha kin blame her. A' that depravity.
Men's filth and dirt and beerie breath.
Rank wey tobacco and stale herring.
Folk used to come by Christian Sanderson
to keep clean. I did a guid honest wash.
I didnae mak much. Onybody can find a tub. Soap.
My dochter wis starving the day o' the clockmaker.
Ten years auld and licking her lips like a cat.

There wis a frowzy blight on the window panes.
The gas lamps were blawing light on the auld toon.
The clockmaker was well abune the mu
when I knocked him doon and rifled his trousers.
Bell sat on him, pinned his airms. Tickled his chin.
I ran my big laundry hands thru his pants.
But his big cape, tho' fu o pockets,
had nae notes, jist a mouldy old sandwich.
Dirty swine! Bell and I had to share 16 shilling.
Bell wis that disappointed she wis blazing:
'Bloody stupit rich auld fool coming oot
wey no money.Hardly a blastit fortune.'

Man robbery. Robbery from the person.
Seven years.Transportation. Australia.
It's a long word. *Au stra li a.*
When I heard my sentence in Edinburgh
I just aboot passed oot.
They said I wis a thief by habit.
What kin o habit's hungry, bony?
I got hot around the back o my heid. Dizzy.
I wondered whether I'd survive thon
terrible boats they pit you on
or if I'd arrive in the upside doon
lan' deid an dun. 'The mulatto's a thief by repute.'
That word I hate – mulatto. The Mulatto this,
the mulatto that. I felt like saying,
'My name is Christian Sanderson.'
I kept ma lips pursed thegither.
I looked doon at ma broon hands, crossed ma fingers.
Whit's going tae happen tae my dochter?

If that drunken clockmaker
had no remembered
I'd no be in this position;
or if I had decent employment at onything.
I wid hae worked if I could ha found it.
I'm no shirker.I wid hae sweated in ony workshop.

Men that make clocks remember things.
Women that suffer sullen poverty want tae forget things.
At the end of the lang day nothing's worth sixteen shillings.

Gambia

The day I go into the witness box
I am better dressed than I've ever been:
white linen –
white linen dress, white linen headgear,
and I wear
about my neck a filigree necklace.

I am a kitchen maid, I say. I cook. I clean.
I am thirteen. I go by the name
Gambia. I have no other name.
Gambia. My master travelled the gold coast
and brought me back to the bungalow.
I never had wages, No.

I have never been to school.
My mistress tore up my Book, my bible.
I saw all my prayers burn in Hell.
She laughed and the fire crackled and spat.
I knew something bad would happen like that.
It was midday and the sky was ash grey.

My mistress asks me if I said something.
I said yes. When I came to this country
I was taught to say yes. Yes is good manners.
She said that word, honour. Her honour.
But I don't know what honour means.
Then she beat me with her husband's walking stick.

The crook at the end hurt me the most.
It hurt me inside my body.
The blows didn't pain me.
She held up my clothes and beat me
then she stepped on my back, my mistress.
My back was bad. I was in distress.

I was screaming and I could hear my screams
coming back to me like ghosts.
I could not get up. I lay face down.
After that the cruelty man came, looked at my body.
My mistress told him she will flog me
every minute every hour every day

that I don't obey her. She say,
'I'll please myself' to the cruelty man.
But she didn't say that in the witness box.
She had to sit down. Her face was wan.
She was crying. She told lies with words and looks.
Lies she told, even though she swore on the book.

I don't know if they believed her,
or if they believed the cowkeeper.
I keep his good look in my heart, here.
I am going away to some other place.
I don't know where.
And I heard they did call it cruelty.

And I heard they did call it cruelty.
I smiled to myself quietly.
I fingered my fine filigree.
My mistress will doubtless think twice
before she flogs, beats, cracks
the back of a girl like me.

Lucozade

My mum is on a high bed next to sad chrysanthemums.
'Don't bring flowers, they only wilt and die.'
I am scared my mum is going to die
on the bed next to the sad chrysanthemums.

She nods off and her eyes go back in her head.
Next to her bed is a bottle of Lucozade.
'Orange nostalgia, that's what that is,' she says.
'Don't bring Lucozade either,' then fades.

'The whole day was a blur, a swarm of eyes.
Those doctors with their white lies.
Did you think you could cheer me up with a *Woman's Own?*
Don't bring magazines, too much about size.'

My mum wakes up, groggy and low.
'What I want to know,' she says, 'is this:
where's the big brandy, the generous gin, the Bloody Mary,
the biscuit tin, the chocolate gingers, the dirty big meringue?'

I am sixteen; I've never tasted a Bloody Mary.
'Tell your father to bring a luxury,' says she.
'Grapes have no imagination, they're just green.
Tell him: stop the neighbours coming.'

I clear her cupboard in Ward 10B, Stobhill Hospital.
I leave, bags full, Lucozade, grapes, oranges,
sad chrysanthemums under my arms,
weighted down. I turn round, wave with her flowers.

My mother, on her high hospital bed, waves back.
Her face is light and radiant, dandelion hours.
Her sheets billow and whirl. She is beautiful.
Next to her the empty table is divine.

I carry the orange nostalgia home singing an old song.

Yellow

The hedge has its hair cut and stands between us
and the neighbours. The crocuses' yellow tongues
try to talk. The yellow bird in the birdcage is let out –
sometimes it flies alarmingly into my nest of hair.
I dream of budgies born in my curls. My mother
takes the yellow-and-white checked tea towel
from the kitchen and weeps into it before
drying the dishes; but she never cries into
the tea towel that is the map of New Zealand,
the south island, the north island, Christchurch, Wellington.
Never weeps into that one. My father, on the phone,
barks at cowardly comrades, *Now look here Comrade!* My brother
plays his flute in between chirping Not listening Not listening.

When my aunt Peggy comes from Edinburgh, she shoves my head
into a runny yellow yolk and says, *Don't be fussy! Get that down you!*
When my grandmother comes, my mother rushes up the stairs
and throws up in the bathroom. When my grandmother leaves,
my mother says, 'She always has that effect on me.'
Then we eat, my mother and I, her on her empty stomach,
eat what she calls *a plate*, 'Shall we make a plate?
Cheer ourselves up?' The plate has passionate beetroot balls
rolling across it, a piece of Edam because it's slimming,
a slice of ham, a happy yellow pineapple ring.
Two white sweet pickled onions stare like blind eyes.

Whistle Down the Wind

My brother has his fingers,
dirt under the over-long nails,
on the tin whistle
he doesn't know how to play.
Its sharp insolent notes
speak for him
since he is an adolescent
and adolescents don't talk or listen.

I am not yet one of those, but can't
imagine me not-talking, but then
I am, according to my brother,
Miss Goody Two Shoes.

Suddenly, he rises up from the armchair
where he has been sitting,
screaming out the spiteful folksongs
of his own making;
takes his whistle
and, for no good reason, whacks
me straight across the face.

My mother is up on her feet,
pushing him and he is falling backwards
as my mother screams *her face you've got her face.*
I've got no face.
My brother has got my face in his hands,
shaking it back and forth.

My face is rubber; sly as a mask.
He's in trouble this time.
Big trouble. The sting of tin is sweet after all.
Big big trouble. I feel myself laugh under my ice jaw.
My two shoes get gooder and gooder.

But he never was.
Big Trouble never arrived on its noble horse
with its long whip to save me.

Oh whistle and I'll come tae you my lass.

Bleep

I am the unreal voice speaking.
I will not be told I am real.
I care for the inauthentic, the disingenuous.
Deceit makes me shiver with glee.
I fall for false tears, false modesty,
false eyelashes, false teeth.
I enjoy seeing them sitting in a mouth
watching a soap on TV, pearly
as Hollywood can be, big white falsies.
Square, unreadable and slightly odd.
Wigs with synthetic hair, I hold dear.
Plastic hips. Silicone chips.
The wee tuck here and there.
I adore the plucked eyebrow,
shocked and bare, feigning surprise
at you there. I dote on everything false
from the moment I wake up from my faked sleep
for the rest of the fabricated day.
Bleached skin, shrunk arse,
wee tits, tiny hips, nae chin.
There's nothing like women faking it.
See my nose, it used to be a tomato.

Virus **

nose eaten away
flesh scaly
mutilated fingers, toes.

wearing the sick dress,
ringing the bell as warning –
not well, dead among the living

not well. living hell.
there is the imagining
there is lust/sin.

now much later
the word shakes you up.
leper.

as if 'colony' = fiction.
leprosy: a terrible imagination.
black fingers; trying a hand at it.

Fiction

When I first try my hand at it,
my character moaned
not just for a day and a night, but
for three solid years.
A voice in my ear, groaning,
whinging, whining, whimpering,
sighing big heavy heaving sighs. Up and doon. Huh.
Puffing, oot of breath, *For crying out loud.*
She was a martyr – snivelling, Scottish.

Fed up, grief-struck, going on and on and on
and on: how she was the mug, the sucker,
taken-for-granted, how I could see *her* coming,
take her to The Cleaners. *Oh Dear.*
As for that man of hers, well he wasn't a man at all.
On she went, too close. The voice in my ear.
Heigh-ho. A widow's voice, weeping in the wee small hours,
weary, poorly, all in the one relentless tone.
The same sorry pitiful moan.
'I've had it,' she'd say, 'Up to here.'

But she had no neck, no body, no face, bonny or raw.
She had no hands to blaw her nose
with a big white hanky.
She had no eyes to cry out,
teeth to gnash or hair to tear out.
She couldn't remember.
'Gie me peace?' she'd say.
'Does onybody ever think o' gieing me peace? Naw.'

One day I climbed up my steep study steps,
my heart dead, my own voice shaky and ill with it all,
paranoid, spewing self-pity,
thinking this fiction will kill me.
Up I puffed, seized by a sudden fury
to kick the life into her.

There was a blue glow in the corner.
There she was, curled on my floor, at the back,
by the attic door, covered with my father's old coat,
breathing, her face slightly flushed, shy, black,
her body plump and surprisingly fleshy.
I fell to my fat poet's knees and cried holy.

The Birth and Death of Bette Davis

On her way down
the birth canal
she shouted,
Fasten your seatbelts it's going to be a bumpy night.
She came out
smoking a cigarette saying,
I never ever want to do that again.
In the room was a pale nurse and a silver bowl.
Oh – and a momma.
In the bowl was the placenta, lush purple stuff.
Make this into puff pastry placenta pie
and feed it to my father,
she said, and then sucked for a moment on her mother.
One second was enough for her.
Goddamn, fetch me a gin,
she roared at the feeble midwife.
She flicked her cradle cap, tossed her single curl.

*

It was the one part
she never wanted:
one day she went out looking for her looks
and lost them.
Her skin was lined, bad dialogue on cellulite.
Her eyes were covered in film.
Her bow and arrow eyebrows were stuck in a tree.
In the room was a man
who never loved her, the bastard.
He told little lies under his coat.
She swore at him and fought the morphine
Her last line was her first.

She had the stars.

False Memory

It came to her when she was out
walking and it stopped her dead.
She must have stood there
for a lifetime like a tree
rooted to the spot,
her thin arms jabbing the wind.

Don't tell me it is not true.
His hair is falling over my face.
I can still see him
coming through the crack of light
at the bottom of my room,
splitting me open like a nut.

For a long time she blotted him out.
She didn't know why her mouth spluttered
wet, nervous laughter
after each time she saw him or why
she hid him tucked up in the hem of her skirt
or why she scrubbed the back of her neck.

I would love him to be false,
no flesh or blood, no shadow or beard,
no looming booming presence in a room,
to be all lies, fake, fiction, sham.
A bit of her would rather not remember;
but when I did the memory was a flood

pouring itself out, murky and green
all the riverbanks swollen, gushing
incidents from my life, his face, my face
the dark all lit up
and suddenly my small house
was floating on the water.

I saw myself, nine years old,
shipwrecked, soaked, floating down
the river with the lovely name,

the name I can't speak,
without filling again, as if the
river was my childhood,

as if I could say I was
down by the river with the lovely name,
and none of it happened;
it didn't happen because I was busy.
I was busy fishing for tadpoles or trout
or watching dragonflies
or looking for interesting debris –
a new word I had just learnt and loved to use.

Life is full of debris
I would say to my girlfriends
and none of it would have happened.
But one night it did.
And then it happened again.
And then it happened again.

The focus blurred, blunt edges,
a family album, grins and grimaces.
The dark developing night.
Now I can peel back the wet
pages, and let her out,
carefully. I won't damage her head.

From Stranraer, South

Looking back, I can say, with my hand on my heart
that my mother got sick the day I said I was in love
with a girl who lived round the corner –
and never got better.

So Aileen McLeod left the day after my mother collapsed.
She caught the afternoon train from Stranraer, south.
My mother wouldn't open her mouth –
and never got better.

Friends brought me news of Aileen, here, there,
and she herself sent me two letters.
The first said come now; the second don't bother; yet my mother
never did get better.

I don't know if it's me or if it's her, but I'm sure
a certain expression of satisfaction crosses her cheeks
when I give her a bed bath, as if she's taught me a lesson –
it will never get better.

I see myself in our hall mirror smiling my mother's smile,
complicit, apologetic, I know what you're up to.
No matter what I do I can't wipe that look from my face.
It will never get better.

I carry in holy water. I lift her head. Tilt her chin.
I dab round her smile with soft flannelette.
I bring the commode and stroke her hand. Fresh sheets.
It will never get better,

better than this, for what is a life for but to be a good daughter
and love your mother's weakness and moisten her lips
and listen to the sound of her dreams in waves
and see the stars outside flicker and waver, uncertain.

Bed

She is that guid tae me so she is
an Am a burden tae her, I know Am ur.
Stuck here in this big blastit bed
year in, year oot, ony saint wuid complain.

There's things she has tae dae fir me
A' wish she didnae huv tae dae.
Am her wean noo, wey ma great tent o' nappy,
an champed egg in a cup, an mashed tattie.

Aw the treats A' used tae gie her,
she's gieing me. A' dinny ken whit happened.
We dinny talk any mair. Whether it's jist
the blethers ha been plucked oot o' us

an Am here like some skinny chicken,
ma skin aw bubbles and dots and spots,
loose flap noo (an yet as a young wuman
A' took pride in ma guid smooth skin.)

Aw A' dae is sit an look oot this windae.
A've seen hale generations graw up
an simmer doon fray this same windae –
that's no seen a lick o' paint fir donkeys.

The Kerrs have disappeared, but the last
Campbells ur still here so Am telt –
tho' hauf the time A' dinny believe her:
A've no seen ony Campbell in a lang time.

My dochter says 'Awright mother?'
haunds me a thin broth or puried neep
an A say 'Aye fine,' an canny help
the great heaving sigh that comes oot

my auld loose lips, nor ma crabbit tut,
nor ma froon when A' pu' ma cardie tight
aroon ma shooders fir the night drawin in.
Am jist biding time so am ur.

Time is whit A' hauld between
the soft bits o' ma thumbs,
the skeleton underneath ma night goon;
aw the while the glaring selfish moon

lights up this drab wee prison.
A'll be gone and how wull she feel?
No that Am saying A' want her guilty.
No that Am saying Am no grateful.

Virus ***

No that Am saying Am no grateful.
Am aye grateful tae ma hosts,
awratime, and if by ony chance
ma host the rat snuffs it,
A kin a ways switch tack.
Big man, wee wuman, wean:
it's awrasame tae me.
Don't get me wrang,
Am no aw that choosy,
as lang as the flesh
is guid and juicy.
One bite and Am in,
one bite and they're mine,
in the neck, the groin.
Whit! Ma success rate
is naebody's bisness.
Wey ma canny disguise
A make sure human hosts
drap like flies.
Bubo! It's all go.
O sweet Christ.
Sweet blood bodies.
Somebody's dochter. Somebody's Maw.

Maw Broon Visits a Therapist

Crivens! This is jist typical.
When it comes tae talking aboot me,
well, A' jist clam up. Canny think whit
tae say.

Weel, weel. A'm here because
A' canny hawnle life, ken whit A' mean,
because everything is awfy
and A'm no masell.

A' dinny ken who Maw Broon is anymare.
A' canny remember ma Christian name.
A' remember when A' wis a wean,
folks cried me something.

The idea o' me ever being a bairn
is impossible. A' feel A've aye worn
this same pinnie and this heid scarf
A've got on the noo.

How come you've no got anything tae say?
You've no opened yir mooth.
Whit's wrang. Am A' no daeing it right?
A' dinny ken hoo yir supposed tae dae therapy.

Jings. Dae A' jist talk on like this?
Michty. This is awfy awkward.
You've no said a dickie bird.
Tell you a dream? Crivens,

A've no had a dream since A' wis a wean.
An image? Whit kind of image?
What comes tae mind?
Whit represents whit?

Och. This therapy's making me crabbit.
A' thought this wuid mak me happy.
This is awfy. A' feel unweel.
How dae A' see masell?

Weel. Am fed up wey ma bun.
It is jist a big onion
at the back o' ma heid.
A' canny let ma hair doon.

A'm built like a bothy, hefty.
A'm constantly wabbit and crabbit.
Ma hale faimily taks me for grantit.
A'll aye be the wan tae dae it

whitever *it* is. Here – A'm quite guid
at this therapy lark eh?
Here, Maw Broon could be a therapist.
Sit there like you are, glaikit,

a box o tissues and a clock,
a few wee emmms and aaas.
Jings, it's money for auld rope.
There that's whit A' feel like –

a tatty auld rope
nibiddy wuid want tae climb
a' twistit and tangled
an, jings, this is exciting

A' could break. A' could jist give in.

Room

I don't know what the room really looks like:
it is dark, the curtains almost drawn in daytime.
A suspicion of strangers steams up the windows.
The tall lamp hides behind its coy fringes.
A glass table is as transparent as you are.

You turn your slim gold ring round and round,
as if you wished you'd made another decision –
or is it me who thinks you should think that way?
A patterned scarf around your neck, loosely.
You think your neck is fat and thick.
Your soft lips are parted, slightly open.

So when you wash your face,
when you take the flannel and wash your face,
when you rub the cloth across your broken veins,
the simple act of it brings tears to your eyes.

Interior

In the room where the sun is down
and the light is sad and frail,
vulnerable,
lighting up a lone apple on the table

where the heart is dressed in heavy wool
and the old woman in the young woman
that I am is waiting for her time,
sadness is well-mannered, quiet, soft.

Characteristics of Sadness

A sad face has extra eyebrows:
thick, furled – small winter animals;

A third eye that weeps when the twins are dry.
A thick lazy tongue.

A running nose, a long distance champion.
The sad skin has a tinge of green.

Sadness on a face is full of character.
It could be literature
or it could be a movie star
or it could be great art.

But right now in this house, it stinks.

It can't be blamed on the season.
It is spring. There is honeysuckle.
(Even that has a sad sweet smell)

Perhaps it has its uses.
It could be made into something else.
Recycled. Carried out in blue boxes.

Or mixed with sourdough.
Or changed into running ink.
Or used as a mask to frighten away friends.

Which gene is responsible?
Who passed it on?
Who is to blame?

You. You'll do.
You sad bastard.
Cut the snivelling you sap.

Josephine Miles House

You had a fence built around this house
so that nobody would spy on you,
but I am living inside your house
                              spying on you.

I have found signs in your old books
William Butler Yeats *Autobiography*
squiggles at certain passages and codes:
R, N, 904, P. All pencil. 1946.

In the bathroom the steam is sad.
And in the dark lightless study
the gloomy tree is anxious
outside the window, its thin

branches fretting about something.
Some days blinds fall down
without pulling any string.
Once I was certain you turned out all lights

till I ran out into Virginia
and saw all houses dark, quiet.
I stare at your smiling face in the hall.
I think I know you:

witty, clever, acerbic, sad.
Life and soul.
I use your gassy cooker,
your old yellow sink.

You never used them yourself.
Yesterday a letter arrived for you.
Your name in my mailbox,
as if you were still alive.

I walk out past the squashed camellia heads
lying in your front yard like dead fruit
up Virginia into Arch
saying your name, saying your name again.

I see you being carried up the steps of Wheeler
by your attendant students, like a Queen of Poetry.
There are things I tell you daily.
Things I hear you tell me, a continuity.

Love Nest

The mice come first. In our bedroom
at the top of the house we hear the cunning
scraping, scuttling inside the skirting.
It is the first sign.

The plague of flies is next. In our kitchen
at the bottom of the house, they swarm in sick
thick circles. It is late October.
The Pied Piper calls. 'Something big,' he says.
'Must be something big and rotten.

Look for the eggs, tiny, white.'
This is the time of the Wests.
'Do you mean a body?' you say, anxious.
The Dalston train thunders by like fury

At the bottom of our town garden.
And yesterday the wasps came.
Two thousand strong. An army in my study
and the wee toilet. The Pied Piper returns.
'Vicious bastards,' his eyes gleam with job satisfaction.

This is our love nest. I see you, looking at me.

Virus ****

Our love nest.
Your love nest.
Their love nest.

Thrush first. VD. Crabs. Lice.
Gonorrhoea. Syphilis.

A kiss on my belly first.
A kiss on her belly next.
A kiss on my belly last.

Church Invisible

And because he once said,
My belly was set about with lilies,
He set about to beat me.
And because he once said
My navel was a round goblet,
He turned my stomach.
And because he wore a collar,
No one suspected him.

And because I was unworthy,
He grew to loathe me.
And because I worked hard,
He despised my rough hands.
And because I was his wife,
I submitted to him.
And because I failed myself,
He punished me more.

And because he became angry,
I saw his fury everywhere.
I could feel the colour
Of his rage on my skin.
And because I was beaten,
I was moved out of my house.
And because I was battered,
I was driven out of my Parish.

For he is the Lord in the Lord's place
And I am his servant.
I am she who looketh forth
At the morning, fair as the moon,
Clear as the sun,
Terrible as an army with banners.
I am she who cannot stop
Seeing his raised hand.

Husband

Your husband's eyes are out of it,
the eyes of a guy who has never known himself
and is surprised –
his hair is receding like the tide.
Only the fish he catches know him and they die.

Paw Broon on the Starr Report

Right Maw, hen,
if that man can
get it wey a wuman
that's no his wife,
I'm hauving it wey you.
I've aye been loyal.
There's no use in you
saying 'Naw Paw' again,
Christ, the President
gets it, so so kin I.
Get yir heid doon wuman,
an hae a guid sook.

Christ, wait a minite.
I'm no a lollipop.
Dinny lick gingerly,
it's affy tickly,
gie me a guid sook! C'mon C'mon.
Haud on! Let me
position masell.
Wisnae the President
staunding agin a wa'
or wis it the lavvy door?
Wait till ma back's pressed
up agin it. There. That's perfect.
Whit the Hell's wrang noo?

Sabbath

I

I wake, gargling my holy bells from village to village to town.
I bathe in the small slice of river that has become my own.
I cross a field of corn; a dead tractor; the farmer's silent scythe
holding a still mouth of hay. I pass the milk-barn where each holy
        cow mutters
a rosary, along the country road where hedges sit opposite
like believers. Down by the cottage a woman wakes in a fit
and washes her hands. The weekday broom fasts, starved of dust.
There is nothing stopping me. I walk in big strides, as I must,
across this land – curtain after curtain opens, the relief of confession.
My church is grey. My people are clean. I shake their hand for
        morning mass.
The light in the sky is divine. I dedicate myself to the sun.
Every tavern has a bolt. Every village shop has a shut door.
Every bolted horse has a shut stable. Bad luck strikes with one chord.

Come lunchtime, I feed them. No day will boast a better roast:
golden potatoes, honest gravy, roasted parsnips; I'm a good host.
Before the food they will always thank me, or be cursed.
Nothing worse than my scowl, my scorn, my thin lips pursed.
If you can't be good on my day you will wish you never were born.
Standing solemn in the Square are the good children,
born on my day with meek, bonny smiles on their faces,
dressed in their Sunday best: crease in the trouser, check in the dress.
Satisfied here, I head for the town. Up the steepest of hills,
the smell of praying like the smell of chicken is comforting. I inhale
deeply, this cool noon. The mist on the hills,a christening shawl;
the wind keeps up with my pace the way a faithful dog will.
Nothing to match one of my walks. I pass people,
hand in hand, arm in arm, alone, past the church and steeple
and nod and tip my hat, say Good Day, Good Day and have
        Good Day said back.

II

Not in a month of myself did I ever imagine change.
Years pass. I punish those who sin. I have free range.
The wife of the hunter who fornicated on my day
has a baby with the head of a dog on the 7th of May.
Sometimes I choose the best punishment of all – forgiveness.
Sure as fate they will pray themselves out of the mess.
Finally, in the late afternoon, I head for town.
My eyes sore. Cars cough up phlegm.
The steeple beckons with a crooked finger.
I pass a man, sick in the street, who is my dead-ringer.
My own reflection rears up in a mirror. I am growing thin.

Shop doors are shamefully wide. I am all in.
Lads by a dull corner swig brown beer. Jigging music
swirls from alehouses. I feel faint, sick.
I go into one. 'I am the seventh day,' I shout.
Some big fellow bangs a gong and chucks me out.

III

I run backwards , my tan leather shoes skidding on the cobbles.
The sky stained with the red of cocktails.
The stench of the city in my hair; my clothes stale.
Smoke and stinking sewers. My own breath tastes of ale.
Quick – down the terrace where no child goes to Sunday school,
where arguments ring instead of bells and some man's cruel
shadow punches his fist against a wall, blasphemous.
There's the man who shouts obscenities. Infamous.
I can't stop myself; I mutter his curses under my breath
trying out the new fierce words. Quickstep.
All the colour drains from the sky like blood from a face.
The street suddenly darkens. In one house, I see a woman's face
bruise. A man closes the curtain. No one sits with the book,
no one clasps their hands in prayer. No one gives a kind look.
I am ill; I feel my own blood thin and weaken.

IV

I am lost. Dim eyes. This dark street is the same as the last.
My legs are losing their power. I have lost my past:
the deep secretive lanes of my childhood,
the barn, the bales of hay, the good moods.
I try to speak to myself: all I get back is gibberish.
A bad dog skulks past without a leash or a wish
for an owner. I follow it till I come to a corner, turn left
and up the hill. The smell of dung makes me feel bereft.
I am losing my senses. Everything has changed.
I am not at home; every house has been rearranged.

V

A big dish give me the cruel eye
from Ballantyre Farm. The old Square is crammed with lies.
Pious hypocrites; selfish people who would not share a meal.
My feet are heavy wooden crosses. My full lips are sealed.
Nobody recognises me. I am invisible in my old hometown.
Not a single greeting. No choir boy in a proud gown.
It is half past eleven. My collection box cannot sing.
No musical threepenny bit. My stricken bells cannot ring.
My back is bent. Somebody, somewhere has put me to the test.
Sing a hymn. I am done. I am no better than all the rest.
Darkness. Rock me to sleep. I have lost my elegance.
One last lullaby. One wistful, parting glance.
Adeste Fideles. Agnus Dei. Angelus Domini.
Anno Domini. Amina. Alter ego. Lapsus Calami.
I vanish to the pinpoint of my own dark eye.

The Broons' Bairn's Black

(a skipping rhyme)

Scotland is having a heart attack
Scotland is having a heart attack
Scotland is having a heart attack
The Broons' Bairn's Black.

Pride

When I looked up, the black man was there,
staring into my face,
as if he had always been there,
as if he and I went a long way back.
He looked into the dark pool of my eyes
as the train slid out of Euston.
For a long time this went on
the stranger and I looking at each other,
a look that was like something being given
from one to the other.

My whole childhood, I'm quite sure,
passed before him, the worst things
I've ever done, the biggest lies I've ever told.
And he was a little boy on a red dust road.
He stared into the dark depth of me,
and then he spoke:
'Ibo,' he said. 'Ibo, definitely.'
Our train rushed through the dark.
'You are an Ibo!' he said, thumping the table.
My coffee jumped and spilled.
Several sleeping people woke.
The night train boasted and whistled
through the English countryside,
past unwritten stops in the blackness.

'That nose is an Ibo nose.
Those teeth are Ibo teeth,' the stranger said,
his voice getting louder and louder.
I had no doubt, from the way he said it,
that Ibo noses are the best noses in the world,
that Ibo teeth are perfect pearls.
People were walking down the trembling aisle
to come and look
as the night rain babbled against the window.
There was a moment when
my whole face changed into a map,
and the stranger on the train
located even the name

of my village in Nigeria
in the lower part of my jaw.

I told him what I'd heard was my father's name.
Okafor. He told me what it meant,
something stunning,
something so apt and astonishing.
Tell me, I asked the black man on the train
who was himself transforming,
at roughly the same speed as the train,
and could have been
at any stop, my brother, my father as a young man,
or any member of my large clan,
Tell me about the Ibos.

His face had a look
I've seen on a MacLachlan, a MacDonnell, a MacLeod,
the most startling thing, pride,
a quality of being certain.
Now that I know you are an Ibo, we will eat.
He produced a spicy meat patty,
ripping it into two.
Tell me about the Ibos.
'The Ibos are small in stature
Not tall like the Yoruba or Hausa.
The Ibos are clever, reliable,
dependable, faithful, true.
The Ibos should be running Nigeria.
There would be none of this corruption.'

And what, I asked, are the Ibos faults?
I smiled my newly acquired Ibo smile,
flashed my gleaming Ibo teeth.
The train grabbed at a bend,
'Faults? No faults. Not a single one.'

'If you went back,' he said brightening,
'The whole village would come out for you.
Massive celebrations. Definitely.
Definitely,' he opened his arms wide.
'The eldest grandchild – fantastic welcome.
If the grandparents are alive.'

I saw myself arriving
the hot dust, the red road,
the trees heavy with other fruits,
the bright things, the flowers.
I saw myself watching
the old people dance towards me
dressed up for me in happy prints.
And I found my feet.
I started to dance.
I danced a dance I never knew I knew.
Words and sounds fell out of my mouth like seeds.
I astonished myself.
My grandmother was like me exactly, only darker.

When I looked up, the black man had gone.
Only my own face startled me in the dark train window.